MACAW CARE GUIDES

A Typical Guide Book On How To Take Proper Care Of Your Macaw. Know Their Behavior, Types, Habitats, How To Groom And Feed Them

MIKE WILLIE

Table of Contents

CHAPTER ONE

INTRODUCTION

Macaws are pretty outstanding searching, they are clean to apprehend with their large heads, sturdy curved beak, and a stylish long tail. They are also very clever and inquisitive birds, and they're additionally lively and playful. Being tremendously wise and very social, they want plenty of interest and toys to preserve them busy. Pet Macaws adapt well to captivity, adjusting without problems to their cage or aviary and their new domestic. A younger macaw will tame quick and bond to its keepers.

The feather coloring of the macaws is colorful and delightful. The maximum familiar sorts of macaws are big birds though a there also are a few species, known as mini macaws, which are medium, sized. Irrespective of what their length, they're all captivating birds.

The huge macaws generally tend to have the maximum unusual feather coloring. Mini macaws are mainly a brilliant inexperienced with a few shade accents on their shoulders or tails. Some of macaws had been cross bred, producing quite a selection of hybrid macaws. The hybrid macaws have remarkable variations on the regular coloration in their parentage.

Macaws make excellent pets however are very loud. They may be now not the best talkers, however they love socialization. Social interplay is the important thing, a puppy macaw may additionally soon begin to mimic the sounds of their keeper's voice as well as many different sounds in its environment. Macaws are incredibly wise as well as each energetic and interactive, making them very outgoing and brief to pick out up on tricks. A blissful lifetime partner for the right keepers!

TYPES OF MACAWS

The natural Macaw species are usually broken into two organizations, the massive Macaws and the Mini Macaws. Mini Macaws are people who handiest attain up to about 20 inches (50 cm) in overall period. There are 8 living species (together with subspecies) of Mini Macaws and eleven living species (plus several subspecies) of big Macaws. Huge macaws are brilliantly colored at the same time as the smaller macaws have a tendency to be predominantly inexperienced.

Incredible versions of the normal hues are achieved through hybridization or cross-breeding as opposed to the mutation of a species. Hybrid Macaws had been produced in captivity, and this became often the result of coincidence wherein two species of macaw have been kept inside the equal surroundings. They might become near companions, bond and then produced offspring. Due to the contemporary interest and recognition of those birds, hybridization for the puppy trade has resulted.

Hybrid macaws are frequently very lovely birds with wonderful coloration. Some styles of hybrid macaw are now 2d or 1/3 generation birds, or maybe more. But, hybrid macaws are still macaws. They may require the same stage of care and dedication from their keepers because the natural macaw species. The coloration of those birds can often be attributed to 1 figure or the alternative, but their temperament and conduct are unsure. for this reason, you may need to examine all you may about each of the parent's characteristic. Make certain you are comfortable with keeping and dealing with all the parent types before acquiring a infant

CHAPTER THREE

MACAW BEHAVIOR

In the wild macaws form a robust bond with some other chook and the pair will join small flocks. In addition they tend to most effective vocalize inside flock situations. In captivity most pet macaws are much more likely to interact with their owners via physical touch, and often use vocal mimicry for interest.

Macaws make remarkable pets. They've very high-quality temperaments and are very playful. A hand reared macaw is usually gentle and without difficulty treated. There are a few matters to be aware of (and to do) in order to have an awesome and affectionate pet macaw:

- Socializing a Macaw

A nicely socialized macaw is a puppy as a way to be loved in plenty of conditions and by means of many human beings for years. A younger macaw must be socialized with as many humans as possible. They also should be exposed to plenty of situations inclusive of new cages, visits to a veterinarian, managing with the aid of friends, and having their wings and nails clipped.

Socializing a macaw and presenting it plenty of studies are the keys to an extremely good puppy. Doing these things will increase a properly rounded chicken that doesn't emerge as worried of recent matters. It'll additionally prevent too robust a bond with most effective one individual developing.

- Macaws and kids

Macaws and children can blend very correctly if the child learns the way to have interaction with the parrot. Youngsters and macaws should be supervised.

- Macaws and Pets

Macaws and other pets also can get used to every other and learn how to accept each different. Again, but, be very careful to monitor all groupings of animals. A macaw can be very dangerous to small pets together with hamsters, guinea pigs, mice, and even small birds. Near friendships are just as feasible as lethal enemy behaviors. You might not understand till the relationship unfolds over the years

CHAPTER FOUR

HOW TO TRAIN YOUR MACAW

Macaws are excellent for taming, and comparatively smooth to train. They're very intelligent, and though fair to terrible talkers, they may be taught many hints. This capacity to research and perform hints makes them a favorite chicken for use in shows all over the international.

Taming and education your parrot relies upon first on believe, so cross slowly and be regular. Keep in mind that taming and education chook takes endurance, by no means 'punish' your parrot! This only serves to wreck the consider you have spent so much time constructing.

- Taming basics

Usually, as with every parrot, you ought to deliver a new arrival a few days to get used to you, your voice and its cage earlier than seeking to handle it. A handfed toddler will now not need tons taming and might frequently be dealt with proper away, as its miles use to human attention.

- Initial Macaw training

Taming proceeds in steps. Your first aim is to get the parrot to just accept a treat from you. This may lead to it permitting you to softly scratching its chest.

Subsequent is hand taming, where your macaw will climb to your hand and can help you convey it round. You may accomplish this by way of supplying it treats from outside the cage until its miles comfortable with your hand. As your macaw turns into at ease with taking treats from your hand, then you definitely open the cage door and repeat the identical process however now you are accomplishing into it is cage with the deal with. As soon as you've got earned its trust, your macaw will start mountain climbing on your hand and allowing you to puppy him.

Relying on the tameness of the chook, these two steps can be immediately as in a handfed baby or take several weeks or longer for an untamed fowl.

•	advanced training

Once your Macaw has gotten over its shyness, then you can paintings on speech and trick schooling. Even though a macaw isn't as exact a talker as the African gray or maybe the Amazon Parrots, they regularly will reply because of their choice for interest and affection. Repetition and frequency are the keys right here. They can be educated to do hints from driving motorcycles to doing balancing acts.

• Macaw behaviors - importance of childhood training

As macaws develop into and via youth they end up more boisterous, mischievous, and hard to address. They must be treated with confidence in the course of this time to hold their appreciate. By no means permit terrible behavior to develop. In any other case they are able to emerge as untrustworthy as a puppy. That is often non-reversible and they may then want to be reserved for breeding in preference to as a puppy.

FEEDING YOUR MACAW

Right bird care for Macaws involves more than simply the Macaw weight loss plan. The lists beneath cover Macaw meals and dietary supplements as well as information about feather preservation with bathing and grooming.

Macaws are a very excessive strength bird and for appropriate fitness they'll want lots of right ingredients wealthy in oils and energy. Within the wild the bigger Macaws consume a spread of palm nuts while the smaller Macaws devour seeds, nuts and fruit. Each macaw, relying on its size, will devour approximately 1/2 - 3/4 cup of parrot blend and approximately 1/2 - 3/4 cup of fruit and greens.

- **Chicken meals**

Foods to be had for Macaws encompass formulated diets, both pelleted or extruded, seed best diets, and parrot mixes which offer a mixture of both. There are professionals and cons to feeding most effective a formulated weight loss program in addition to feeding simplest a seed weight loss program.

Formulated eating regimen

A formulated diet gives an amazing nutritional base so does no longer require the addition of vitamins, however it does no longer include the phytonutrients (antioxidant pigments) which are located in vegetables, end result, grains, and seeds. Phytonutrients are believed to reinforce the immune system, assist a body to heal itself, and to prevent a few diseases.

Also, parrots can become bored with it because of the lack of variety.

Seed weight loss program

A seed best weight-reduction plan offers a whole lot more range however requires additional diet and calcium dietary supplements. Macaws need now not best nutritional requirements met but additionally variety for psychological enrichment.

A Macaw food plan including a terrific parrot blend which incorporates formulated ingredients, an expansion of seeds, dried end result, and nuts is commonly seemed as a suitable base to offer vitamins and variety. Alongside this, offer an everyday complement of fresh fruits and veggies.

- **Supplements**

Culmination and vegetables

Supplemental meals include all varieties of end result such as apples, pears, plums, cherries, grapes, oranges, bananas, mangos, papayas, or even berries consisting of strawberries and blueberries are enjoyed. Many veggies consisting of carrots, sweet potatoes, cucumbers, zucchini, darkish inexperienced leafy vegetables, many lawn greens, and even dandelions and chickweed are desirable. Do not feed avocado as it is able to be toxic to birds!

Treats

Provide nuts for treats, which includes macadamias, walnuts, pecans, almonds, and filberts.

Proteins

Additional proteins may be offered together with sprouted legumes and cooked hen or meat.

Grit

Grit is not taken into consideration important as macaws will shell their seed before ingesting it.

- Water

Give your macaw fresh ingesting water each day.

- Bird Baths

The private hygiene of your Macaw includes a regular bathtub or bathes for appropriate plumage and pores and skin circumstance. One way to perform this is with either a handheld bathe sprayer or a hose with a fine spray head and lukewarm water.

CHAPTER SIX

GROOMING YOUR MACAW

In grooming your macaw, you must learn how to do the following:

Wings

The wings have to be stored trim if you need to deter flight and to prevent the lack of your puppy via an open window or door. Clip maximum of the primaries (10 feathers closest to the wing tip) and simplest sufficient so the bird can waft to the ground.

Beak

The beak wishes to be trimmed if it becomes overgrown or deformed. There are many mineral blocks, lava blocks, and other beak grooming items available at your pet store to assist your hen preserve its beak in form.

Nails

a selection of concrete kind perches are also available to help the hold nails trim, but they ought to be trimmed in the event that they emerge as overgrown

CHAPTER SEVEN

MACAW HABITAT

- fowl Cages

A Macaw cage ought to accommodate a totally huge parrot. Provide the largest fowl cage possible. A macaw need to be capable of fully make bigger its wings without touching the edges of the cage. The largest macaw, the Hyacinth Macaw, has a wing span of 3 - 3 1/2 of toes. Macaws ought to also be capable of pass freely among perches or muscular dystrophy can arise with the intention to render it unable to fly.

Every other very vital attention is that macaw cages be very durable. These birds are very strong chewers. Macaws are also very good at beginning cage doorways, so make certain the cage has locks or break out-evidence latches.

• Hen Perch

Offer perches which might be clean fruit tree branches, they're remarkable as your hen will like to bite on them, and of course they will need to be replaced regularly.

The branches want to have a few areas which can be approximately 3/4 in diameter, and even bigger diameter areas for large macaws.

• Hen meals, deal with, and Water Dishes

It really works best to have the dishes putting from the side for feed and water. Attempt to vicinity the perches faraway from dishes so the food and water dish do no longer come to be soiled with bird droppings. Do now not use plastic due to the fact your chook will chunk and break the plastic and it could come to be unsafe.

- Macaw Playpen

A playpen is good for playtime outside of the cage. it is a essentially a massive, unfastened-standing perch with food and water bowls, and places to grasp toys from. Commercially made Macaw playpens usually have a tray under them as nicely, to trap something dropped to the ground.

- Macaw chook Toys

Playthings may be things like hiking ropes, chains, bells, parrot swings and timber or different chicken toys. Destructible toys are right due to the fact they may be "interactive" so assist relieve boredom, but non-destructible toys will last longer. Macaw toys may be highly-priced.

• In which to area a Macaw Cage

Due to the fact macaws are very loud, the quantity of noise and the closeness of buddies should be considered while determining wherein to hold you bird. Macaws are very social and inquisitive, so the room you house your pet in may be a room that gets visited often by means of the own family. Vicinity the cage at eye level in a quiet sunny region away from drafts.

- Housing renovation

The basic cage care includes each day cleansing of the water and meals dishes. Weekly wash all of the perches and dirty toys. The floor has to be washed about every other week. A complete hosing down and disinfecting of an aviary ought to be completed yearly. Update something that wishes to be freshened which include vintage dishes, toys, and perches.

CHAPTER EIGHT

HOW TO BREED MACAW

It become not till the early twentieth century that reviews of macaws breeding in captivity were launched. Even nonetheless, only a few birds have been efficiently bred at that point. This is probably due to the fact they are difficult to sex and because most imported birds have been kept in my opinion as pets.

• Nowadays the wide variety of macaws being bred in captivity is extensively changing. This is because of a decrease in imports and due to the growth in call for these extremely good birds. Nowadays maximum of the birds bought as pets are captive bred. Numerous Macaw species are simply available in the pet industry as handfed babies, and extra are becoming an increasing number of to be had.

- Sexing Macaws

All macaws are sexually monomorphic. This means the intercourse of macaws can't be reliably decided by way of physical traits, even though the males are usually larger with larger heads.

Their sex need to be decided through either a surgical probe referred to as endoscopy, which may be executed with the aid of many veterinarians; by way of DNA checking out, usually a blood pattern or some plucked feathers dispatched to be identified in a lab; or a chromosomal evaluation.

- Pairing Macaws

Macaws breed simply but the sexes have to be confirmed and the pair must be harmonious, bonded with each other.

It is nice to let them macaws choose their personal friends. This is great performed accomplished inside the iciness more than one month before breeding season.

The appropriate breeding ages are 4 – 8 years, with a maximum breeding age of 30 - 35 years for the most important macaws.

- Breeding environment

Macaw breeders will need a nest container. The macaw's nest box desires to be approximately 3 instances the macaw's body duration in height and one body period in width and depth. The hole desires to be simply big enough for a person to go into.

There needs to be some blocks secured in the field for the birds to climb out and additionally numerous blocks of wooden on the inner partitions for chewing. Provide 4 - 8 of wooden shavings within the backside of the nest container. Mount the next field high up in a corner facing outwards, an area that offers seclusion and safety.

- Egg Laying and Hatchlings

Most macaw species lay clutches of two - 3 eggs. The larger macaws will lay an egg each other day and the smaller macaws will lay every 1/3 day. The incubation length is 26-28 days. As soon as the hatchlings are born the mother and father will want a ready supply of food and particularly like corn on the cob, sparkling fruits, milk soaked bread and cuttlebones. The weaning stages from 10 weeks to 8 months, relying at the species. It takes 16 or extra weeks for the young to fledge.

CHAPTER NINE

MACAW HEALTH CARE ISSUES AND LIFESPAN

A macaw this is properly cared for will seldom grow to be ill. But there are some sicknesses they can contract and there are some environmental things which could motive illness. There also are behavioral issues that they can expand. Even though it's miles frequently hard to decide contamination, some seen signs of contamination to be conscious. Here is a list of factors to be issues to be privy to, a list of symptoms that imply an ill macaw, and what to do if your macaw will become ill of his behavior troubles.

A number of the greater not unusual illnesses seen in Macaws:

•	Proventricular Dilation disorder (Macaw wasting sickness)

•	Psittacosis (chlamydiosis or parrot fever)

•	Bacterial, viral, or fungal infections

•	Feather choosing - results of boredom, bad eating regimen, sexual frustration, and lack of bathing

- Allergies

- Chewing flight and tail feathers through juveniles

- Beak malformations in chicks

- Papillomas

- Kidney disorder (gout)

- Toxicity - heavy metallic poisoning

- Lipomas in older birds

Visible signs of a sick Macaw

- Ruffled plumage

- Listlessness

- Drooping wings

- Sagging frame

- Intense mood modifications

- Having no appetite

- Bulges in feathering

- Partially closed or watery eyes

- Swelling of the eyelids

- Rasping

- Issue respiratory

- Immoderate saliva

- Grimy vent

- Any exchange inside the feces now not apparently weight-reduction plan related

What to do when you have a unwell Macaw:

- In case you see any signs that make you suspect you have an unwell macaw, immediately location it in a warm, draft loose, cozy environment.

- maintain it at about 86°F (30°C).

- Vicinity meals and water near the perch where it's far without problems available.

• An ill parrot has to be taken to an avian veterinarian for analysis and treatment as soon as feasible.

• Behavior problems usually stem from something lacking within the chook's surroundings. Boredom, lack of accepts as true with, loss of interplay with different birds or human beings can lead to problems like biting, feather plucking, and screaming. Attempt to expand a bond of believe and spend time with your chook to assist keep away from these issues.

Macaw Lifespan

How lengthy do macaws stay? That is a crucial query that macaw fanatics ask. Macaws are often mistakenly notion to live as much as 75 years or greater, but this is inaccurate. The actual lifespan of a large Macaw and Hybrid Macaws is among 35 - 60 years. The lifestyles span of the Mini Macaw is shorter, on average they will live 20 - 25 years. Macaws aren't as long lived as the cockatoos. A 40 vintage macaw will start displaying the symptoms of growing older and a 50 year old macaw is a totally old chicken!

THE END